Heart Container

Marian Kent

Also by Marian Kent

Responsive Pleading
SUPERPOWERS or: More Poems About Flying

Copyright ©2015 by Marian Kent
ALL CAPS PUBLISHING
All rights reserved.

ISBN 978-0692589458
(ALL CAPS PUBLISHING)

Cover design by Max Germer.

Title font is Luna by Amanda Leeson.
Author photo by Aaron Meuse.

*Dedicated to the memory of my grandmother,
Anne Gilmore Stewart*

Contents

Belly

What to Do When Pain Recedes	3
Bellyball	4
These Feet Were Made For	5
Wishbone	6
Map of the Body	7
Go West	8
Now It's Dark When You Leave Work	9
After a Broken Heart	10
Fine for Littering	11
Your Headlights Are On	12
12 Minutes or a Lifetime	13
Duck & Cover	14
Sobriety	15
Winter Affirmations	16
Boiled Over	17

Backyard

To Summer Vines	21
Bile	22
Dandelions	23
Early Civilizations	24
Mirror	25
For Sylvia, By Moon-Light	26
The Moon, From the Bathroom Floor	27
Forget About Those Revitalizing Creams	28
Bees Get Rowdy at Sunset	29
Castles in the Air	30
Go Back for Your Gloves	31

L'esprit de L'escalier	32
Autumn Blues Insist on Orange	33
Evidence of Something	34
Nocturne	35
Stridulation	36
Alice	37

Dresser Drawer

If Not Now, When?	41
Land of the Lost	42
Turn Around, Bright Eyes	43
Practice Limited to Horses	44
Fluidiosyncracies	45
Last Chance Gas	46
Mitchell's	47
Buy One Lilac, Get Two Bearded Iris Absolutely Free!	48
The Farther City	49
Dali's Bend	50
Words, or Lack Thereof to Describe	51
Send in the Clowns	52
Mosaic	53
Memorial Day	54
Songs of the Great Indoors	55
April	56
Spring Wins Again	57

Jelly Jar

Trouble With	61
On Commuting	62
What Happened at the Oxbow	63
Untitled (Eight)	64

How to Feel When Shit Gets Heavy	65
Gray-Pink	66
Plea to the Gods in Charge of the Sunset and Other Things	67
How Many Licks Does It Take	68
City of Homes	69
Beanstalk (Optional)	70
Queen-Sized	71
Traps.	72
Hidey-Hole	73
Magic vs. Tragic	74
Cartography	75
Love in the Time of Astronauts	76
Pressure Drop	77

Notebook

Shot in the Back	81
The Price of Milk	82
With a Bit of Tremor in My Hands	83
She Wishes to Loosen the Verse-Grip	84
Shadow's Song	85
Desperation	86
In Which She Takes Time to Reflect on Time	87
One Thing Facebook Sure As Hell Is Good For	88
How They'll Find Us	89
Some Dreams	90
Hooked	91
Rocket Ships	92
Aphorism	93
If Wishes Were Typewriters	94
Waiting on Parades	95
Acknowledgements	97
About the Author	99

Belly

What to Do When Pain Recedes

The skin covering my shins
is starting to heal, long-held
bruises fading to translucent, scabs

less prominent, soon gone smooth
like your singing as I wander
dream-sidewalks not lost at all

casually, no longer requiring
awakening from stifled screams.
Soon our city will shine bright

and green even at night, birds
will awaken us from the monotone
of March, you will smooth your hands

up my thigh and notice it is healed.
I will thank you for singing, for your
rapt hands expelling night terror,

a lifetime of bruising below the surface
of things. Give me your hands and sing.
Let me give good thanks for the healing.

Bellyball

Ball in my belly
bellyball
poised
to hurtle downlane
& crash
wrecking ball
waiting
for a straddler
ball & chain
the whole ballawax
bloody moonball
in my belly
about to be eclipsed

These Feet Were Made For

Looking down in the shower
I can see my feet

It wasn't always so, years
of carrying babies and all that followed
conspiring
so I never paid attention
to my feet anyway

Now my feet are wiser
witnesses
supporting struggles and my noticing
every small thing

Including my feet below my belly

Wishbone

A history of my hips
fiercely jutted in defiance,
then submitting.
Swaying, waxing with child
pliably bearing
war-tugged just shy of splitting
but always springing back.
Reaching, striving
circumnavigating
the expanse of you—
(I will meet you here. I can
hold you here.)
Wilted, still unbroken,
the enervation of years
you read in my hips.

Map of the Body

Torn creases,
raggedy-edged,
stuck
with yellowed tape,
directions
fading in the ocean
of my arms, push pins
locating
future pain points
along the organ corridor,
beginning with the heart.

Go West

October blows
like a cherry bomb
in a maple sky,
spreading out
pandurate
against gooseflesh,
pining for wool.
October greets
seven with the lights on,
heads west,
rounds
the autumn-scattered curve
where your friend's son
breathed his last crisp
fan of night,
already wishing for spring.

Now It's Dark When You Leave Work

Once you notice the ghosts
in your rear-view mirror, you're stuck
with them. They follow you home.
After that initial clench of fear
in your belly, you get used to them.
They become comforting, even.

It's because you dropped that fortune
cookie fortune from your purse
on your way out, then picked it up:
>   *You are alert to the events*
>   *and feelings around you.*
The ghosts know that is true and smile.

They're why you didn't run over
that raccoon running back and forth
in front of your car. They are with you
at night, and they wake you in the morning.
They notice, too. They notice blue.

After a Broken Heart

You feel the impact,
holler *Oh hell no!*
But yes, it's happened
like something you might read
in a novel synopsis
on a dust cover jacket-flap
but it happened to you,
no pretending.

After the yelling
and sorting-out of things
there's a thick ache,
pounding paranoia,
the body memory of crash
written on your spine
as though inked there
with white-hot needles.

Fine for Littering

Unfurled
burger wrapper
lit on my windshield
in an instant I saw it all—
the crash
the decapitation
body parts strewn across the highway
my husband receiving the news
presented with a bouquet
of severed limbs
my wedding ring
no ceremony
motherless
children.

Your Headlights Are On

Poverty, poverty
with all the passion of the sun
awash in pennies practicing
lazy heliolatry
bowing down round
and round

Heavy, heavy
flesh-colored feldspar
illuminating fog-fallen lanes
bent with branches
wheel-gripped worrieder
and worrieder

12 Minutes or a Lifetime

I am trying to write a poem
about a twelve-minute window
allowing witness to depravity
perpetrated by youth
against weaker youth
but the violence is so extreme
it begs the question *what have we done*
for which I have no answer
fit for poetry
Meanwhile I'm preoccupied
with wondering what it would feel like
to be impaled from the inside
from the part of me reserved
for entrance by express invitation only
To beg for life
but to die
Where does the pain start
and how does it end

Duck & Cover

Chug
your water
with devotion

Hold
the wine
in your mouth

Lay
your expectations
across my nape

Express
your belligerence
in tight phrases

Sobriety

Listen to sullen songs
    Breathe through swollen lips
  Wallow in missing Things
You have no business
    Considering
  What you have to lose
That you'd choose Imagined
    Bruises on pinkest lips
      Is too much to contemplate

Winter Affirmations

You said
head north to go south
so we ringed the Fingerlakes
in a blizzardy fever
staring straight ahead in case of deer
crossing

Plastic bags waved in maple branches
translucent
like rice paper
or prayer flags
rice noodles searching for cucumbers
seasons away

You said I love you
as we approached the river
numb
considering the currents
still rushing under layers of ice
and my inferior vena cava

If we sink
there's a supply in the trunk
canopic jars especially for afterlife
but keep my heart intact
true north
promise

Boiled Over

Our eyes met across my belly
and a stack of pancakes
then batted down again
covert
We were spies
in the house of held grudges

Steam rose from boiling sap
like hair on the back of my neck
as boots scuffed muddy gravel
familiar laughs echoed
then dissipated in a sugar cloud
Who were those people?

The line for maple products
was a dozen strong
and everyone looked guilty
I forked potatoes in anger
You observed it can't be healthy
to grow resentment alongside a baby

So I let the baby go

Backyard

To Summer Vines

I'd like to lie here in the shade
    clematis twining round
the maple trunk, then round my arm
    tethering me to Ground
        And you
    wrap round me like you do
        No harm
    befalls us as we lie
No fear of hair braided in blades
of grass, our patch of Sky.

Bile

Yellowed by pollen and regret
nails gnawed to the quick
not quite remembering that dream
but for a fragment

Knifing poetry
on a picket fence

The lilacs are intoxicating
insistent as they annually are
on celebrating all of Spring's
failures to thrive

Dandelions

Suddenly dandelions
everywhere we looked,
in front yards and side yards,
wide meadows, town commons,
that strip of grass
between sidewalk and street—

It was so quiet
as everyone noticed
dandelions
unapologetically yellowing
all that green
with only birds trumpeting
praise for dandelions,
we were too stunned to sing—

In the quiet
we could even hear bees
thrumming
dandelion pollen,
considered dandelion gratitude
as bees
don't have it easy these days—

Then we remembered our machines,
the place of dandelions,
and obligingly
started our engines.

Early Civilizations

The kind of June
that's caught off guard,
when love goes low
in the wake of all that rain.
You are left picking violets
greedily,
gathering large bunches,
hoarding against catastrophe.

Mirror

If you lay
cheek to the ground
you can observe
spectres of your losses
rising from blades of grass.
What you are witnessing
is your own decomposition—
an odd thing to realize
as pill bugs tickle your bosom.
I will be watching
from the crotch of my maple.
Look, my heart hangs
from the uppermost branch
waiting for you,
wishing it could reach,
latch on to the crescent moon,
bring you along tonight,
last night,
probably tomorrow as well.

For Sylvia, By Moon-Light

In a wish for barren Night
or light or want of foresight,
unbelieving she'd be seen
between the Moon and a dream,

Unleashed, her callous fervor
set lust against lust once more,
but more is not what it seems
when begging the Moon for dreams.

Too soon her spit uncovers,
flits away from Light, lovers,
and Night indulgence to breathe
where the dampish Moon meets dreams—

She might wish for simple dreams,
but Moon-dreams aren't how they seem.

The Moon, From the Bathroom Floor

Listless
your pale-cold brow
swollen tongue
& vomit-crust
in the corners of your mouth

roused by silence
to fixate on the moon
peeking through what you wish
was Sylvia's yew tree
instead of your staid maple

how romantically
bald-blue tile
cradles your head
which
if you had the strength

in the blackness
to shift 90 degrees
would give you a sightline
through the door
into the kitchen

& a snap
of the oven
so you close your eyes again
giving over
to the murmur

Forget About Those Revitalizing Creams

I want to age
with natural beauty
like the craggy maple,
red with buds, scraping sky,
briefly belying the lush to come,
cradling the moon
before blanketing him away
from pining eyes.
No one questions
the value
of the blessed maple,
the squirrels keep her playful,
and each year offers another chance
at achieving perfection.

Bees Get Rowdy at Sunset

I don't have a snapshot
of your face as it appeared
the evening the bees turned on you,
but I can see you,
one eye swollen shut,
cheeks puffed as though with acorns
hoarded for a long winter.
What to do when your bees attack
while you're alone
and when I get home
you realize you're even more alone?
What is there to do,
sizing one another up
through eyes swollen with the rage
of bees and want, sunset over
the apple tree that's turned on us—
once an evening
marriage-tree in a stolen meadow,
now the saddest light
in a swollen year
of bees.

Castles in the Air

Fruitless raking
has me musing on you:
there's a reason
for all those songs
about girls
with the wind in their hair.

Draw the rake,
observing the empty space
between elbow and rib,
how cold fingers
are the stuff of autumn
in your absence.

Hoist another rakeful
onto a pile,
make-believe turrets and garrets
stormed in a burst
of every day this year,
blowing leeward.

I hear your laugh
in a circus of sparrows,
hang up my rake,
remembering
there's no controlling wind,
no controlling you.

Go Back for your Gloves

Conserve resources! Peeled
off jeans tugged-in long johns
buttoned-again advice
to approach fear with toasty
extremities. Likely
leaves of last year blown
bide their decay under sootsnow
like gravelly guards while sun
takes a breather out back.
Backpedal to downgrade public
admonition in favor of strange
looks like a smokestack lists
after decades of disuse. Wonder
whether common squirrels feel
the ache of possibilities bygone
or judge us for our tendency
to ill prepare. I guess
it's too late to marry an architect.

L'esprit de L'escalier

It's like the mountain
dressed for company—
red ascot & cummerbund
atop an earthy tuxedo,
pine cologne, and a fresh
clean shave for the holidays.
And the view is spectacular!
How they've opened up the place,
exposing the staircase
with intricately carved rails
rising from a grand foyer,
inviting all of us to dance.
The magnitude of this party
overwhelms your sense of size,
puts you in your place—
just a guest in a Metacomet gala,
imbibing at the pleasure of the Queen.

Autumn Blues Insist on Orange

This is the season
for writing about itching,
wondering where last time went,
second-guessing sins.
Forever on your hips! cries
the cinnamon cider donut;
northerly mistral
wafts pumpkin spice so pungent
you're belly-achin' already.
Horoscope predicts
bad decisions will take roost
unless you atone
for a season of slacking—
lackluster at best, at worst
facing headwinds whirling
with decayed branches.
Not much to do about autumn
but pray that sucker out, waiting
for the first fruit-fly frost.

Evidence of Something

Today's the day
for cleaning up after squirrels
tossing green branches on a pile
fanning spindly strings of smoke
rising from the backyard bonfire

I'm considering tossing on my books
bras & slips of paper stashed inside
recipes for insurrections all of it
fueling the slow poisoning
of the neighborhood through cracks

Upstanding nuclear family facade
& wide-open windows that'll teach ya
to keep your front door deadbolted
against random signature collectors
& altruistic fumigators

There's this tickle under my arm
& my lemonade tastes funny

Nocturne

In the backyard darkest night,
bougainvillea speaks to me;
Or perhaps the wild rose hedge,
cuckolded yet somehow free—

Bright light exits, whispry tunes
sung alto, brushed with whiskey;
Only this hour resonates,
trembly limbs are somehow free—

Lover, I will follow you
through inky night, faithfully;
Risking falling overboard,
drowning amber, somehow free—

In the backyard, darkest night,
somehow free on trembling knees.

Stridulation

We might
shut the window,
but then we'd miss
the rhythm of katydids
and passing cars.

If we closed the blinds,
the pulsing streetlight
would not throw
hashmarks
across my thighs.

Alice

You lit
like butane
creased
on a Snyder chair
trembling like papers
rolled with a jones
Yet
held your ash
held it still
steely
steady gaze
past my ear
Held my breath
prayed
for it to drop
counted by Mississippis
till it crumbled
You toked Death
for so long
when it came
I was unprepared

Dresser Drawer

If Not Now, When?

Whatever this is
is whatever it was,
was exactly right
right then.

Then whatever for
for whenever if,
if the time is now
now's a long time away.

Land of the Lost

In those lost days,
crayfish pooled under the bridge
for the erection of mud motels,
kids fished the crick & burnouts
climbed trusses threatening
to jump, someone'd yell *Kinger!*
as a German shepherd lapped the yard
& a shirtless girl'd prostrate
herself on the sticky-hot blacktop
of the one-lane bridge, wailing
come'n get me my days are all done!
daring cars to run her over.

Turn Around, Bright Eyes

Now that I think about it,
that clubhouse might have been
just a dilapidated Sears shed,
circa 1960-something.
To us, it was a posh teenaged haven,
benches and windows suspended
on chains for hanging out.
I never saw any teenagers in there,
but the evidence of their coolness
was painted on the door:
KNOCK THREE TIMES.
By the time we were teens ourselves,
we rejected the clubhouse confines.
Maybe it was torn down,
or maybe the clubhouse was a boy thing.
We, after all, were girls,
out tanning in the backyard,
radio blaring from stereo speakers
pointed out a bedroom window
when the DJ interrupted a Foreigner song
to announce: ANDY KAUFMAN IS DEAD.
We gussied up for the prom anyway,
slow-danced, rewinding the words
to Total Eclipse of the Heart:
Every now and then I fall apart.

Practice Limited to Horses

Today, idling
at a traffic light
I notice the sign again:
VETERINARIAN,
Practice Limited to Horses.

As though it's 1977,
I watch from the window
as the guy in the plaid
and chaps
strides up to the colt
tethered in the side yard,
embraces his hind quarters
(contrary to what I know
about never approaching
a horse from behind),
man-handles his colt-cock
(whacking down there
with what looks like
my mother's garden clippers)
and chucks something
over the bank into the crick.

That was the day
the colt became a gelding.
Today, I remember
the benefits of staying calm
and on my best behavior.

Fluidiosyncracies

A man
admonished his lover
for wiping her counter
with a dish towel
while baking
egg whites are like snot
he said
then fucked her
on the same counter
His own kitchen table
hoard of crusts and papers
cursive letter
why won't you have me
I would forever sit naked
reading your magazines
smudged
photo of a smiling girl
leather couch cushions
wiped off
with a dish towel

Last Chance Gas

Let's travel to the sliver
where sky meets the road
out beyond the neighborhood
just past that morsel of river
studded with glacial potholes
all shimmery shiny & shit—

Bet we can be there by tomorrow
away from the sorry here of here
in throes of the garbling
misty-winged throes of beyond
but in tomorrow's tomorrows
where could we possibly go next?

Mitchell's

In the milk bar
of my imagination
we sip malts & gossip
about who has the freshest lapels
trade ideas for hemming
& appliqué
You suggest I could take in my blouse
by an inch or so
to better show off
my God-given natural assets

In the dive bar of memory
you announce to the room
that we're Together
to fend off stumbled advances
then we drink & drink
& drink
until we stumble ourselves
out in the street
to your dive apartment
where you undress in front of me

And dive into your bed
leaving me to lie restless
too drunk to sleep
on your dive couch
imagining what it would be like
to dive in bed with you
entwined
breathing in your milk-beer sweat
Instead I get up & check the fridge
finding only Pepto-Bismol

Buy One Lilac, Get Two Bearded Iris Absolutely Free!

I remember a septic tank
requiring pumping every month,
wide wooden floorboards
painted grey,
hot-air balloon spotted
in the skylight above the bed,
the 30-inches-of-snow day
and the subsequent river rush.
If I wrote the story of my life,
this chapter would be
long on nature, short on humanity.
But there would be skinnydipping,
kingfishers ratcheting downstream,
peonies.

The Farther City

Lila spun, her skirt blooming
to fill the room with magenta taffeta
like a pregnant peony.

The refinery's best Joes and Bill-Bobs
had hit the canteen for an after-smoke cuppa,
or so they thought.

Most days, New York City
is a world away from this rig,
but here was Lila, making a freaking discotheque
in the coffee station.

Tex stood
at the back of the room
in his enormous yellow trousers,
hoping and wondering.

Dali's Bend

Silhouettes
behind gauzy windows,
foggy outside, across the nether,
wristwatch stopped at the moment
    the curtains parted,
invisibility like a blanket, safety
redefined; perhaps you shouldn't have
prayed for whiskey-scheming
sustenance.

Words, or Lack Thereof to Describe

Your body
hunkered alongside mine
reminding me of parking garages,
take-out pizza half-undressed
    on your sofabed,
midnight woodstove still radiating
like the core of you.
We surface
because hey, it's payday.
You head out for bagels,
tacking shopping lists like nothing could
matter more & of course it does—
    But your matter,
your corporealness hunkered here
your hands covering mine,
short of breath—

Send in the Clowns

A fragile parade
of Emmett Kelly figurines,
clowns on motorcycles,
clowns with puppies & cats,
clowns on picnics with balloons,
watches over the room through curio glass,
poised to sweep up when the lights go down,
always maintaining that tragic smile,
as if to say: *We understand.*
We've seen better days.

Mosaic

Vintage red Fiesta comport
from that thrift shop in Point Breeze,
long ago broken. Quonochontaug
abalone shell, one Roman glass earring
brought back from Jerusalem,
titanium wedding band (inscribed).
Stripes of cobalt-copper Campbell pottery.
Dress buttons, string of pearls,
pewter maple-leaf barrette (keeper lost).
Painted macaroni, empty lip balm tubes.
My children's baby teeth.

Memorial Day

A coverlet of violets
spreads across these hills
to the edge of a lake
you've never seen,
though you are buried here,
deep,
a mirage at the horizon
where the water meets the mountain,
a single poppy
bobbing like a ghost.

Songs of the Great Indoors

Listening to your song
about summer in California
Beach Boys and Spoonful-time
inexplicably brings to mind
a Pennsylvania moment
that probably happened in winter
Billy Idol's sneer
on the big console television
in my grandmother's sitting room
which come to think of it
was a bedroom
I guess she had a 3-bedroom apartment
with a writing desk in that TV room
and another in the living room
though I never saw her writing
at either one
It was the eighties
every season had a White Wedding
Anyway keep on with your summer songs
because it's always winter here

April

by Anne Gilmore Stewart, 1929

When April comes and you are far away—
Bitter-sweet April with her smiles and tears—
When meadows freshened by their winter's sleep
And gently falling rain, awake to find
Blue violets like shy heads among the grass;
When hardy crocus flaunts its gayest hues
Along the paths we loved; arbutus clings
Around our rock up on the farthest hill—
That rock we found last Spring when you were here—
When mad rain swoops across the sky
And leaves a trail of sun behind;
When over all, the soft, sweet breath of Spring
Lies, bringing old memories of you—
My dear, my dear, where April comes to me
With you not here to share—'twill not be Spring!

Spring Wins Again

for Anne Gilmore Stewart, my grandmother

Where once there were layers of grey,
now blossoming violet songs
push against our resistance, strong

desire to keep the grey in play,
shunting suggestion of color
to margins, preferring duller

descriptors for these heady days.
Purples not easily denied
break earth and bloom before our eyes

in majestic Springtime display;
we blink, ruddy-eyed, blink again
attempting to thwart green, but then

the yellows! That first yellow day
warms us, unwittingly joining
the fools who grin at nature's foiling

winter. Another year we stay
for yellows, then reds, and we're done—
No point arguing, Spring has won.

Jelly Jar

Trouble With

Raincoat
    -ing hearts
        cloudburst
-ing other
    wise sunny
        days

On Commuting

Clouds obscuring
kid carrying an amplifier
riding a bicycle
Volkswagen backing into traffic
car ahead refusing blinkahs
but that's okay
I know where it's headed
following blue bliss
all of us like wayward gretels
tracking crumblines
to the clouds
anticipating our last supper

What Happened at the Oxbow

Resisting Spring,
wishing dark clouds
would continue
blocking out the Sun
that tries to warm my hurts.
Why? I ask. I would prefer
to stay right here
under this blanket of clouds.
Crocus replies,
you are looking down.
Lift your face to the Sun,
notice the Eagle soaring high,
inviting you to fly
for another Spring.

Eight

At eight,
she still reaches
for my hand
walking through town
together.

How to Feel When Shit Gets Heavy

Bouncy,
    resilient,
like kicking dreary snow
from weighed-down branches,
    suddenly
airborne.

Gray-Pink

Growl awake
your environs
washed in gray-pink
recall cobalt
thrum of neon
from your core
entwining
missing
but since when
& how about blue?

Plea to the Gods in Charge of the Sunset and Other Things

Toss your tinder
into our crucible,
strike your flint
against the Holyoke range,
smear your chert
across the underside
of our chalkbowl, dusky
as we, insignificant
and tiny below, holler
(like when you bite your tongue,
blood clinging in threads
to the basin edge,
slowly dissipating
in salt and spittle)
remainder us your markings, pure
brilliant red—
We'll awe.

How Many Licks Does It Take

I think of you
while brushing my hair
tugging
gently at first
from the ends up
then impatiently
yanking out the knots
and tossing them aside

City of Homes

Seagulls circle low
over the McDonald's parking lot
as garbage-breeze
wafts from the river,
highway, trash out back the pawn shop.
Window poster declares
The Best Things In Life Are Fries!
It's cool beach-air today—
the gulls are on to something.

Beanstalk Optional

Prophecy recalls
a lark song on your mattress,
& I remember
how your back made a staircase
to a world beyond the clouds.

Queen-Sized

Mattress
on the grassy median
between north & south
near exit 14
bears sunlight
headlights
moonlight
dew & wishes

Traps.

Framed cover
of *Rolling Stone* magazine,
August 9, 1979,
Rickie Lee Jones.

TV tray in the kitchen,
festooned with ripening
cherry tomatoes.

Homemade avocado sushi rolls
with wasabi & ginger.

Wallet on a chain.

Guitar.

Hidey-Hole

That space
between the appliance & the wall
where the dryer lint collects,
where you might find a sock or two,
unmatched.
Sometimes I stuff cookies down there
or a glass of wine,
my kids' baby clothes,
a fraught email,
how I feel right now.
What I don't want to talk about.
I tamp it all down in that crack,
fold the towels,
join you on the couch.

Magic vs. Tragic

Wondering, restless city
Folks turn up the air, hoping
Beyond magical, wishing
For a wandering, so how

Then can it be our heroes
Are not immortal, not now,
Not ever? Nor tomorrow?
Best blessed interloping

Dreams & grand imaginings
Interject grave proportions
into space before revered,

Too clear it's needed, yet feared
The place we rest our fortune
Escapes our bold tragicking.

Cartography

Madly dropping crumbs, forge ahead,
led by that you might've desired,
mired in what could've yet been
when travelling here without a Map.

Mayhap your trail cannot be followed,
swallowed up by birds of prey.
Today you're as lost as you ever were,
bestirred deep down, low moan,

Alone, yet always forward-trudging,
judging not lest ye be mistook—
Look! Yon hawk trains on your pain.
(Strange he can see through you.)

Eschew your modern-life concerns,
learn to live without me.
See, the Map's lost its aesthetic—
Prophetic: *I'll always need you badly.*

This poem is inspired by Stephen King's *Dark Tower* series. The italicized line is spoken by Roland Deschain to Susan Delgado in the fourth book, *Wizard and Glass*.

Love in the Time of Astronauts

Love careens pell-mell
across the icy blue stratosphere,
if that's what it takes.

Love defies the laws of gravity,
residing in an alternate dimension
yet to be observed and labelled,
refusing to be contained.

Love carries the ache of scorched
earth and the fathomage of despair.
Love never calls off the search.

Pressure Drop

Wondering whether
you ache with heavy weather
or chew your nails to the quick
though you thought you'd mastered
the trick of catching yourself
before the bite maybe you're
caught in some other sick habit
to help balance the gravity of all
that's pressing and vast
uneasy ballast in a fury storm
starry canines tearing the fabric
of your stories if you stop
to think do you find glory
whipped up with equal parts
gaudy curiosity varied as galaxies
brimming with constellations
or is it just one dull season
after another leaving you grasping
for cosmic adjectives to fancy
up the tedium so you sigh
and make another cup of coffee
I wonder whether you do too

Notebook

Shot in the Back

Write the moon and the stars
and meditation variations
write the songs of horseflies
on compost butterflies lighting
the reediest mullein spike out
back write hope
write the rings
in your maple tree stones skipped
across open water
or hurled in anger
write protest
write songs
rhymes marching shouting cracking
frustrated tears voices
cracking the sidewalk
cracking buckling splitting wide
engulfing voices in awful arrogance
demanding averting but still
but still
you must write it all down
write
it
down
write the abstract crazy
the real of it all
the blood the beaten down how
can this be
the shot how many times of it all

The Price of Milk

I forgot the words
to my own poem

Blearing eyes staring
me down at the sewer-fresh
Misfortune Bar

Unable to fake it
in front of an audience
from the depths

I drowned my verse
in a jug of glitter
and regret

Forgetting to pick up milk
for tomorrow's breakfast

With a Bit of Tremor in My Hands

I'm learning
how words are magical
how writing them down
gives me superpowers
how reciting them aloud
makes the flush rise
from my core to my face
as a woman perched
on a folding chair
watches my lips
words
breath
intoning verse
I know by heart
but read from the page
just to be safe

She Wishes to Loosen the Verse-Grip

Now that you've fairly exorcised
every Demon courting you last
night, last week, or yesterday's lies,
as if your Verses could surpass

The reality of your Truth,
virtue spilled on the page, forecast
cold with a chance of where-are-you
in the simpler Time just gone past

Your prime, your Words resonating
but flying, coming very fast,
sketchily approximating
the Saddest years, already passed

Like yesteryear's iconoclast,
you stay stuck, scribbling down the Past.

Shadow's Song

Life inside a long, long Shadow's
no life at all, one might argue
but would be regretful, sorry
for all that's been forgotten where

My heart settles, comfortable
in the long, long Shadow of you—
I tell myself it's Brilliant here,
bold and unblinking, never blue

But the Dark is light-absorbing,
lurking, watchful, seeking a way
to describe your long, long Shadow—
I follow along, learn my lines

Despite repeating choruses
offering radiance, sun-light,
long nights of summer—I turn and
tune to your long, long Shadow song.

Desperation

Dream
verse
daring
us to seize
the Words they give us
but we hunker down forgetting
    these are the only ones we have
    there are no extras
waiting behind the next stanza
to surprise us with
edited
Words left
for
dead

In Which She Takes Time to Reflect on Time

Before light
& forgot your slippers
drinking coffee for warmth
disinclined to turn the furnace on
that cat expecting something
you don't really have in you
at this hour
but if you can keep the kids asleep
you have a window to ruminate
so you write feverishly
as though time's
running out
because
actually
it is

One Thing Facebook Sure As Hell Is Good For

Sometimes I click
on my page
just so I can see
where it says
you're Married To Me
and then I click
on your page
because it says
I'm Married To You.

How They'll Find Us

Incomplete, like a map
of trails yet to hike,
badges unearned.

Inchoate as scouts
in knee socks
and training bras.

We are Reveille,
We are the Big Dipper.
We are a masterpiece.

Some Dreams

My Love, I will follow you
cross arid paths, the universe,
in your wagon to the Stars—
To you, I will be ever True
deliciously, and never curse
memories uniquely Ours.
Embracing, like Lovers do,
you plus me, better or worse.
Together, we'll keep fear afar—
Some Dreams, it seems, do come true.

Hooked

If crawling 'cross the Universe
is required to show Devoutness,
here I suffer on hands and knees,
proving that Integrity
    ought not be blessed—

Devoted, I shall demonstrate
fruits of Fealty tolerate
thrashing abuse, abundant Loss,
returning only ample cause
    to Celebrate.

Rocket Ships

> Rocket ships
> are exciting
> but so are roses
> on a birthday.
> —*Leonard Nimoy*

Roses deliver
but so does a chicory spray
sweaty-gripped
by a toddler

Diamonds excite
but so do love songs
scrawled in chalk
across blackboard sky

Love's lyric
needs no byline
when adorned with adjectives
tattooed above the heart

The etymology
of our love affair
can be traced from the air
like cropmarks

Aphorism

When all the wrong
songs are awkwardly played,
laid down like liquid tracks,
cracks in sidewalk-sodden Night
rightly forgotten and buried
very deep,
creeping out from under,
wondering why
Sky is empty of color—
duller time'd prevail, you'd guess.
Unless you come to understand,
hand to swollen mouth,
doubted no one then, epitaph
half-obscured: *He Took His Life.*
Might those words be misunderstood?
Should they'd Sing, when they're all wrong.

If Wishes Were Typewriters

You perch
on your desk chair
ballpoint pen to lips
posing
in your natural habitat
pretending
to define poetry
by what it is not

As I
before dawn
unphotographable
in pajamas
coffee
before work-a-day
discover a photo of you
and wish I were Dorothy Parker

Waiting on Parades

My notebook falls open
to a page of ballpoint pen drawings
by my son, who had been sitting
on a curb waiting for a parade.
My own scratchings scarce, inspiration
is welcome when it surfaces.
Who could fail to be moved
by his steady requirement to draw now,
on this curb, on a restaurant placemat,
a napkin if that's all there is?
(Put this in your purse, Mama.)
My children remember the admonishment
of an artist to never stop drawing,
evoking this advice constantly
and with reverence, as though told
from on high instead of under a tent
at the Westhampton Fall Festival.
Obviously, this is a good thing,
a lucky thing, a moment's one-off words
etched deep in the psyche of youth,
the notebook that is life's pleasure,
treasure a mother hopes
will be unearthed over and over,
the mind's riches providing sustenance
for a lifetime of waiting on parades.

Acknowledgements

"Now It's Dark When You Leave Work" was first published in *30 Poems In November! Anthology of Poems to Benefit Center for New Americans 2014*.

"Fine for Littering" was first published in *Hellbent Magazine*.

"Winter Affirmations" and "Boiled Over" were first published in *Tell-Tale Inklings #1*.

"Forget About Those Revitalizing Creams" was first published in *Silkworm 8, The Annual Review of the Florence Poets Society*.

Thank you to Max Germer for illustrating my psyche. I don't know how you do it and am truly, endlessly grateful.

Thank you to Kerry O'Connor and my fellow Real Toads in the Imaginary Garden and to Tommy Twilite and my Florence Poets Society compatriots for invaluable feedback, inspiration, commiseration, and friendship above all. Thanks to Eric Storch, Kirsten Piccini, and John Connolly for talking me off the ledge.

Verses in this volume were inspired by—some readily apparent, others maybe not so much—the work of Wes Anderson, Charlie Chesterman, Steve Earle, Mordicai Gerstein, Stephen King, Ray Mason, Sylvia Plath, Adrienne Rich, Patti Smith, They Might Be Giants, Gerry Yelle, Neil Young, and a checkered tribe of past and present friends and lovers, acquaintances and passers-by. Thank you and much respect to each and every one.

Special thanks to Robert Lipton. *Now you travel that distance, somehow we expect you to report back.*

With all the love to Aaron, Jack, and Anne—my whole world.

About the Author

Marian Kent
Purveyor of Pretty Words and Superheroic Verse

Marian lives in Easthampton, Massachusetts with her husband and two children. *Heart Container* is her third full-length collection of poems. Marian is the founder of the poetry and short-fiction collective ALL CAPS PUBLISHING. Please visit www.allcapspublishing.com. You can find a great quantity of Marian's poetry and other missives at her website: www.runawaysentence.com

To me, fair friend, you never can be old,
For as you were when first your eye I ey'd,
Such seems your beauty still.

William Shakespeare, Sonnet 104

www.ingramcontent.com/pod-product-compliance
Lightning Source LLC
Chambersburg PA
CBHW050915160426
43194CB00011B/2416